DYING FOR ACCEPTANCE

A Teen's Guide to Drug- and Alcohol-Related Health Issues

The Science of Health:
Youth and Well-Being

DYING FOR ACCEPTANCE

A Teen's Guide to Drug- and Alcohol-Related Health Issues

by Joan Esherick

Mason Crest Publishers

Philadelphia

Mason Crest Publishers Inc.
370 Reed Road, Broomall, Pennsylvania 19008
(866) MCP-BOOK (toll free)
www.masoncrest.com

13 12 11 10 09 08 07   10 9 8 7 6 5 4

Library of Congress Cataloging-in-Publication Data
Esherick, Joan.
  Dying for acceptance : a teen's guide to drug- and alcohol-related
health issues / by Joan Esherick.
      p. cm. — (The science of health)
  Includes index.
          10-digit ISBN: 1-59084-847-0
          13-digit ISBN: 978-1-59084-847-0
          1.   Teenagers—Drug   use—Juvenile   literature.   2.
Teenagers—Substance use—Juvenile literature. 3. Teenagers—Alco-
hol use—Juvenile literature. 4. Drugs—Physiological effect—Juve-
nile literature. 5. Alcohol—Physiological effect—Juvenile literature.
I. Title. II. Series.
  RJ506.D78.E846 2004
  616.86'00835—dc22
                        2004012125

          Series 10-digit ISBN: 1-59084-840-3
          Series 13-digit ISBN: 978-1-59084-840-1

Designed and produced by Harding House Publishing Service,
Vestal, NY 13850 - www.hardinghousepages.com
Cover design by Benjamin Stewart.
Printed and bound in Malaysia.

This book is meant to educate and should not be used as an alterna-
tive to appropriate medical care. Its creators have made every effort
to ensure that the information presented is accurate and up to
date—but this book is not intended to substitute for the help and
services of trained medical professionals.

CONTENTS

INTRODUCTION

by Dr. Sara Forman

You're not a little kid anymore. When you look in the mirror, you probably see a new person, someone who's taller, bigger, with a face that's starting to look more like an adult's than a child's. And the changes you're experiencing on the inside may be even more intense than the ones you see in the mirror. Your emotions are changing, your attitudes are changing, and even the way you think is changing. Your friends are probably more important to you than they used to be, and you no longer expect your parents to make all your decisions for you. You may be asking more questions and posing more challenges to the adults in your life. You might experiment with new identities—new ways of dressing, hairstyles, ways of talking—as you try to determine just who you really are. Your body is maturing sexually, giving you a whole new set of confusing and exciting feelings. Sorting out what is right and wrong for you may seem overwhelming.

Growth and development during adolescence is a multifaceted process involving every aspect of your being. It all happens so fast that it can be confusing and distressing. But this stage of your life is entirely normal. Every adult in your life made it through adolescence—and you will too.

Dying for Acceptance

But what exactly is adolescence? According to the American Heritage Dictionary, adolescence is "the period of physical and psychological development from the onset of puberty to maturity." What does this really mean?

In essence, adolescence is the time in our lives when the needs of childhood give way to the responsibilities of adulthood. According to psychologist Erik Erikson, these years are a time of separation and individuation. In other words, you are separating from your parents, becoming an individual in your own right. These are the years when you begin to make decisions on your own. You are becoming more self-reliant and less dependent on family members.

When medical professionals look at what's happening physically—what they refer to as the biological model—they define the teen years as a period of hormonal transformation toward sexual maturity, as well as a time of peak growth, second only to the growth during the months of infancy. This physical transformation from childhood to adulthood takes place under the influence of society's norms and social pressures; at the same time your body is changing, the people around you are expecting new things from you. This is what makes adolescence such a unique and challenging time.

Being a teenager in North America today is exciting yet stressful. For those who work with teens, whether by parenting them, educating them, or providing services to them, adolescence can be challenging as well. Youth are struggling with many messages from society and the media about how they should behave and who they should be. "Am I normal?" and "How do I fit in?" are often questions with which teens wrestle. They are facing decisions about their health such as how to take care of their bodies, whether to use drugs and alcohol, or whether to have sex.

This series of books on adolescents' health issues provides teens, their parents, their teachers, and all those who work with them accurate information and the tools to keep them safe and healthy. The topics include information about:

- normal growth
- social pressures
- emotional issues
- specific diseases to which adolescents are prone
- stressors facing youth today
- sexuality

The series is a dynamic set of books, which can be shared by youth and the adults who care for them. By providing this information to educate in these areas, these books will help build a foundation for readers so they can begin to work on improving the health and well-being of youth today.

1

WHY START?
Reasons Teens
Choose Drugs

I must have been twelve when I tried pot for the first time. I liked it, but I never really thought about doing it much after that, until I started going to a new school. I met some really cool kids and made some new friends who were into pot. I loved getting high with my new friends, so when they invited me to a rave, I went. At the time, my parents were fighting a lot, so when someone at the rave handed me some E, I decided to try it. I just wanted to feel better. It felt so good that I had to do it again. I didn't care about consequences because it was just too much fun and it made me feel like I wasn't alone. It felt really good, until I got busted.

I didn't wake up one morning and decide to become an alcoholic—it kinda snuck up on me; I never saw it coming. I first tasted beer and alcohol at one of my parents' Super Bowl parties when I was only four or five. They thought it was cute when I sipped their drinks. I loved how warm and fuzzy it made me feel. By the time I reached junior

Smoking can become an addiction that is difficult to escape.

high, I could convince my dad to buy me beer. Up until then, my old friends had been part of the "good" crowd— you know, kids that didn't drink, did well in school, didn't smoke or do drugs. But the more I drank, the less fun they were, so I ditched them for new friends who liked to party. My new crowd never nagged me about how much I drank the way my old friends did. They just drank with me. I really didn't think I had a problem—even when I blacked out, or woke up with puke all over my face, or felt so sick in the morning I could barely get up.

I started smoking when I was thirteen because I thought it made me look older, and it was fun to do something my parents didn't want me to do. I never realized that within a year of trying that first butt I'd being doing crack, Ecstasy, speed, and prescription meds. I wish I'd known. Drugs have cost me everything: my friends, my money, my self-respect, my teachers' and coaches' respect, my family's trust, my boyfriend, my memory, and even my freedom. I live at a rehab facility now so I can get treatment—I'm an in-patient at the ripe old age of fifteen. I'm trying to stay clean and sober, but it's really, really hard. I can't believe I was so stupid.

When I was fourteen, I hitched a ride home from school with my seventeen-year-old brother and his friends. In the car, one of them pulled out a joint (I'd never seen marijuana before) and asked me if I'd like to try it. Of course I wanted to look cool, so I shrugged my shoulders and said, "Sure, why not?" So we lit up and passed the joint between us. I didn't know it then, but it wasn't just an ordinary joint; it was a wetstick (marijuana laced with embalming fluid). At first it felt really cool, then it made me feel really powerful and angry. I was hooked after that and couldn't wait to try it again.

> According to the American Academy of Pediatrics, the first drugs most young people try are alcohol and tobacco. These, among others, are called "gateway" drugs because they open the door to other drug use.
>
> ### Triple Threat
>
> 1. Tobacco, alcohol, and drugs affect chemicals in your brain.
> 2. Tobacco, alcohol, and drugs affect other parts of your body.
> 3. Tobacco, alcohol, and drugs affect your thoughts and emotions.

The four fictionalized accounts you've just read are adapted from real-life experiences recorded at the *In Your Own Words* section of the Partnership for a Drug Free America's teen Web site (www.drugfree america.com/Kids_Teens). These stories describe some of the pros and cons of substance use and abuse, its allures and dangers, and several reasons teens start to use drugs.

The fact that teens today take drugs or other substances at all is amazing considering the information available. Drug prevention education programs like D.A.R.E (United States) and D.E.A.L. (Canada) bombard teens all over North America with anti-drug messages. Peer programs like Students Against Destructive Decisions (S.A.D.D., formerly known as Students Against Drunk Driving) and Kids Against Drugs add to the social climate of drug avoidance and intolerance. With fact-based education on substance abuse and its dangers so widespread, you'd expect that drug use among adolescents would decline and that most teens would choose not to do them. Statistics suggest otherwise.

The U.S. Department of Health and Human Services' Substance Abuse and Mental Health Services Administration (SAMHSA) estimates that 26 percent of persons twelve years old and older currently smoke cigarettes (one out of four people, including teens). Despite the fact that underage drinking is illegal, 18 percent of those between the ages of twelve and seventeen currently drink alcohol (nearly one in five teens). Sixty-one percent, or

Dying for Acceptance

Each individual may have a different reason for choosing to smoke, drink, or use drugs—or not.

16

nearly two out of three, young adults between the ages of eighteen and twenty-five are currently regular drinkers. The 2002 National Survey on Drug Use and Health found that 20 percent of teenagers ages twelve to seventeen (one out of five youths) and nearly 54 percent of young adults ages eighteen to twenty-five have used marijuana. The same study also reported that use of cocaine, heroin, Ecstasy, and prescription drug abuse continued to rise in 2002 in both age groups. Despite decades of educational *initiatives* and prevention programs, teens are still smoking, drinking, and doing drugs. Why?

Reasons for Teen Substance Use and Abuse

The reasons behind a teen's choice to smoke, drink, or use drugs vary as much as teenagers themselves. Certainly culture plays a role. In recent decades, American society has become an *instant gratification*, avoid-pain-at-any-cost, do-it-if-it-feels-good culture whose media and advertisements advocate popping pills for even the mildest of ailments. The overwhelming sense of *entitlement* and self-gratification so prevalent in our culture today tells teens that life is about indulgence—doing and taking what you can to make you happy. And in the midst of this American pursuit of wealth and happiness, we've also seen a decline in moral absolutes: right and wrong have become *relative* concepts rather than the hard-and-fast rules they once were. All these attitudes and values contribute to teens seeing nothing wrong with using chemical substances as a means to feeling good.

17

Dying for Acceptance

In general, however, these six factors seem to be most instrumental in steering a teen's choice away from or toward substance abuse:

- family influence
- peer influence
- circumstantial pressures
- pleasure seeking
- curiosity/boredom
- biological/psychological factors.

FAMILY INFLUENCE

In the second of the scenarios that started this chapter, the young alcoholic started drinking as a youngster during his parents' Super Bowl parties. His parents drank; they affirmed his drinking; using alcohol, even in excess, was an acceptable part of family life; and his father purchased beer for him. Research indicates that 80 percent of children's values, morals, and attitudes are formed by the time they reach the age of eight. This teenager's values about alcohol were well molded by then and established for years to come.

The fourteen-year-old in the last scenario wanted to impress her older brother and his friends. Here again family influence opened the door to substance abuse. Siblings, cousins, parents, aunts, uncles, grandparents—all can greatly influence a teen's decision about drugs.

Sometimes family influence starts at a much younger age. It can even start before birth. We've all heard stories of babies born addicted to cocaine because of their mothers' crack use during pregnancy and of infants born with fetal alcohol syndrome (FAS), a set of physical, mental, *neurological*, and behavioral birth defects that appear in babies whose mothers consumed alcohol during pregnancy. Though these conditions are completely preventable, infantile addictions and FAS affect these children for life. According to the National Organization on Fetal Alcohol Syndrome (NOFAS), FAS has become the leading known cause of mental retardation and birth defects.

Drug Use and Crime

According to the National Institute of Justice's Arrestee Drug Abuse Monitoring Program (ADAM), 83 percent (eight out of ten) of all prisoners scheduled for release in 1999 had been using drugs or alcohol at the time they committed the offenses for which they had been incarcerated.

In the case of FAS, a parent's actions cause addiction in her unborn child. In our two scenarios, a parent and an older sibling modeled and approved of substance use, which led to those teens' later addictions. But family influence doesn't have to be negative. A 2002 study released by the National Institute of Child Health and Human Development revealed that parental involvement in early adolescence can actually overcome peer influence when it comes to smoking. Researchers found that teens whose parents were involved in their lives were less likely to start smoking than teens who did not experience much parental involvement, regardless of whether or not their parents were smokers. *Involvement,* not smoking status, influenced teens more.

Not every kid who comes from a smoking or drug-abusing family becomes a smoker or an addict, however,

Exposing the Myths

MYTH: Everyone uses drugs.

FACT: The Substance Abuse and Mental Health Services Administration (SAMHSA) found that 15.9 million Americans ages twelve and over used illicit drugs in the month preceding their 2001 National Household Survey. That represents only 7.1 percent of the population, or less than one in ten Americans of that age. Nearly 93 percent of that population did *not* use drugs.

nor does every kid from a nonusing family stay clean. Something beyond family influences must impact a teen's choice to do drugs.

PEER INFLUENCE

Many teens will tell you that friends are the most important things in their lives. Having friends, being accepted, fitting in, being liked—these are all very real needs for all people, even grown-ups, but these needs are especially real for teenagers. The less confident a teenager is about who he is and what he believes, the more pressure he's likely to feel to be like everyone else.

In this chapter's first scenario, the teen who ended up busted initially had no interest in pursuing marijuana use after he tried it the first time—until he moved to a new school and wanted to fit in. Drug use was his way of meeting, making, and fitting in with new friends. Leaving

Peer pressure plays an important role in the decisions teens make.

his old school left him uncertain and insecure about his social standing, and the desire to be liked was so strong that he'd do anything to be accepted by the new school's "in" crowd. His lack of confidence left him far more vulnerable to new peer influences than he had been at his old school.

CIRCUMSTANTIAL PRESSURES

The Ecstasy user of our first scenario went to a *rave* and tried E for the very first time because she was tired of feeling bad about her parents' fighting and she wanted to feel good. This unsuspecting teen experimented with a

Dying for Acceptance

Make your own decisions. Do what is right for you!

The Dynatable™: View First-Time Substance
Users in Actual Time

You can find out how many people are trying
drug substances for the first time every second,
of every day, in real time by visiting the National
Clearinghouse for Alcohol and Drug Information
(NCADI) Web site's "Dynatable" at:
ncadi.samhsa.gov/research/dynatable.
For example, at 9:00 p.m. on Sunday, December
14, 2003, the table looked like this:

Substance	This Year	This Month	Today
Marijuana	2,482,832	106,132	6,252
Alcohol	5,369,934	229,545	13,523
Heroin	137,299	5,869	346
Cocaine	1,106,023	47,278	2,785
Hallucinogens	1,517,922	64,885	3,822
Inhalants	1,072,652	45,852	2,701
Cigarettes	2,825,127	120,764	7,114

Teen Drug Use Increases with Age

The National Institute on Drug Abuse's (NIDA) Monitoring the Future study (MTF) found these trends in U.S. high school drug use in 2002:

Substance	Percentage of 10th-graders who have tried or used in their lifetimes	Percentage of 12th-graders who have tried or used in their lifetimes
Illicit Drugs	44.6	53.0
Tobacco	47.4	57.2
Alcohol	66.9	78.4

harder drug than she'd planned on ever using because she wanted to escape her pain. She also used the drug because it was there—it was simply available.

The National Institute on Drug Abuse identifies parental issues, ready drug availability, and poverty—all circumstantial pressures—as three key factors that put a teen at high risk for choosing to do drugs. Without problems, teens would have little reason to want to escape.

Without drug availability, teens would be unable to get the drugs they wanted, if they wanted them. Adolescent *angst* and the ready presence of substances that can be abused make it all too easy for teens to start down the road of drug use.

"Bad" circumstances aren't the only times that drive teens to try drugs. The pressure of participation in sports can lead to drug use. (Think of the track or football star who uses steroids to boost performance.) Heavy academic loads can push overachieving teens to use drug substances to improve the clarity of their thinking. (Think of a student chugging caffeinated drinks to stay up all night studying for an exam.) The desire to work harder, or faster, or longer can lead to using *stimulants* that push the body beyond its bounds.

Trying drugs to get through challenging circumstances leads us to another reason kids start using: it feels good.

PLEASURE SEEKING

Let's face it. People wouldn't continue to use drugs after they tried them if the drugs didn't do something for them. The fact is many abused substances make you feel wonderful, if only for a short while. These substances, we'll learn in the next chapter, often affect the pleasure centers of the brain, creating unnatural feelings of wellness, happiness, and *euphoria*, called a "high." When the high wears off, you're left feeling flat, empty, and dull.

Many teenagers have said that after their first incredible high, their subsequent drug use was an *illusive* attempt to reproduce that first experience. Despite using larger amounts of the same substances, and using them more often, they just couldn't recapture the first feeling. Their pursuit of that initial pleasure kept them coming back for more.

CURIOSITY, BOREDOM, OR THE DESIRE TO REBEL

Many teens begin using drugs or other substances because they are bored and want some excitement in their lives. Some experiment with drugs because they're curious about what the substances will do to them. Others start as a way to rebel against their parents or as a means to test limits.

Adolescence is naturally a time of growing up and becoming more independent. It means discovering who you are and what you can do. Part of this normal discovery process includes a lessening of parental control and a testing of established boundaries. Some teens choose to test the boundaries in constructive, positive ways: they push themselves in sports, they pursue higher academic standards, they become involved in community service, they take on a challenging job. Others test the boundaries with clothing styles, body piercings, tattoos, or statements of personal identity. Still others push the envelope with behavior: arguing, staying out late, slacking off in school, lying, or experimenting with sex.

But for some, substance abuse is their statement of independence. By using drugs they are saying in effect, "See! I can do what I want, and you can't stop me." What many teens fail to realize is that some substances can be *immediately* addicting—after only being used one time. The curious, bored, statement-making teen becomes hooked when she least expects it.

Not all drugs are immediately addicting, nor will all teen drug users become addicts. Many drug users can use drugs now and then for years and never become addicted. Others are hooked after their first or second high. It all depends on the drug substance, its level of addictiveness, and the biological makeup of the user.

Substance Abuse Is Expensive!

According to the Schneider Institute for Health Policy (Brandeis University), in 1995, the estimated financial costs of substance abuse in the United States (including substance abuse-related deaths, illnesses, medical treatment, and crime) were as follows (figures reflect costs for one year):

alcohol abuse: $166.5 billion
smoking: $138.0 billion
drug abuse: $109.9 billion

Biological or Psychological Factors

Researchers have discovered that certain people are more likely to become addicted to drugs than others because of how their bodies are wired. They have a genetic predisposition to addiction; in other words, something about their *genes* makes it easier for them to become addicted than someone else with a different genetic makeup. The fact that many addictions are repeated from one generation to the next illustrates how genes can influence a person's interaction with drugs.

Medical conditions and psychological disorders can also make a person more prone to using and abusing drugs: depression, *bipolar disorder*, *schizophrenia*, *oppositional defiant disorder*, attention-deficit disorder, *obsessive-compulsive disorder*, *posttraumatic stress disorder*, and others. The National Institute of Mental

27

Dying for Acceptance

Health (NIMH) estimates that one-third of those with depressive disorders, and one-fourth of those with major depression, have substance abuse problems as well.

It's Your Choice

Every teen who tries tobacco, alcohol, or illicit drugs, regardless of his reason for doing so, makes a deliberate choice to use them the very first time. A teenager's first use of tobacco, alcohol, or illegal drugs is almost always

Researchers seek to understand the factors that lead to addiction.

Five Reasons to Avoid Drugs Completely

1. Some drugs can kill you the first time you use them.
2. Some drugs are immediately addicting.
3. Drugs affect your self-control; when under their influence you may do something that you'll regret later.
4. Some drugs when taken only once can make you very sick or cause permanent injury.
5. Taking drugs doesn't ever solve problems; it only makes things worse.

a choice. The question each teen must answer is this: are the benefits of using this substance worth the costs?

To evaluate the potential cost of substance abuse, we must understand the risks. To understand the risks, we have to know how drugs work in the body and brain. We'll look at how drugs affect the human body in the next chapter.

2.
THE HOW OF THE HIGH:
How Chemical Substances Affect the Brain

Look at the list below. See if you can discover what these items have in common:

aerosol deodorant
PAM® cooking spray
chewing tobacco
Wite-Out®

marijuana
nail polish remover
spot cleaner
steroids
Coricidin HBP® (cough and cold medicine)
Ritalin®
beer
permanent markers
gasoline
rubber cement
hair spray
morphine
Tylenol® with Codeine
OxyContin®
cocaine
LSD
spray paint

Spray paint can be used to get high.

How Chemical Substances Affect the Brain

Can you guess? First we'll tell you what they *don't* have in common: they are not all illegal; they are not all medicines; they are not all solids; they are not all liquids; they are not all gasses or aerosols; they cannot all be purchased at local stores; they are not all legally available to teens; and they are not all "bad."

So what do they have in common?

- They are all chemical substances.
- They can all be used to get "high."
- They all have the potential to be addictive.
- They all can kill.

Every item on the preceding list, if inhaled, ingested, or injected, has the potential to produce a physical effect in the body. That effect can be good or bad, healthy or unhealthy—depending on use. That is the nature of chemicals. Hair spray, for example, can have the positive effect of taming unruly hair when applied appropriately; but when inhaled repeatedly it can cause heart failure or suffocation. The cough and cold medicine called Coricidin HBP® when taken as instructed can ease the runny nose, sneezing, and cough of the common cold; but when taken in very high doses can cause hallucinations, seizures, brain injury, and death.

Some of these chemicals have legitimate uses that were never intended to include anything relating to the body: spot removers are chemicals designed to break down the compositions of tough-to-remove stains; gasoline is a chemical designed to be highly combustible to produce power for combustion engines; rubber cement is a chemical designed to be used as an adhesive. Each has a positive, productive function when used as intended; but if used as a means to get high, these can chemically alter the body in ways that can cause permanent or fatal injury.

In that sense, every item on the list could be considered a "drug": a chemical that produces a physical effect by changing the way the mind or body works.

What Are Drugs?

Teens often try to rationalize smoking cigarettes, drinking beer, or inhaling paint fumes as being "okay" because they think they are not "doing drugs." In one sense they are right; they are not, strictly speaking, taking medicines. But in a larger sense they are wrong: tobacco, alcohol, and inhalants are all chemicals that alter brain chemistry, just as more typical "drugs" do. By the broadest definition, the term "drug" can include any chemical substance that changes the chemistry or *metabolism* of the brain or body.

How Do Drugs Work?

Jerome takes a slow, deep drag on a joint. He takes another, then another. Slowly he begins to feel relaxed and spacey; then he gets hungry. He's experiencing "the munchies."

Natalie looks at the yellow smiley-faced pill in her hand and, at the urging of her friends, pops it into her mouth and washes it down with a big gulp of bottled water. Thirty minutes later she's convulsing on the floor.

Steroids are used to "bulk up" muscles.

Mark jams a needle of anabolic steroids into his thigh once a week to bulk up his muscles and increase his strength. In just a matter of weeks, his moods begin swinging between depression and rage, and his face erupts in acne.

What's happening to these teens? Each one is ingesting a chemical: one is inhaled, one is swallowed, and one is injected. All three are experiencing a chemical's effects on their brains and body—each chemical causing a different set of effects.

To understand how drugs affect the body and why different drugs do different things, we have to first look at the brain and how it functions.

Dying for Acceptance

Imagine you are the captain of a nuclear submarine. In order to operate your submarine effectively, you have to man the control room where you receive information from command team members stationed at instrument panels in the control room with you and from other controllers in distant parts of the sub (for example, the engine room, the rudder control room, the sonar room, the torpedo room, the maneuver room, the mess hall, the cabins, the store room). You and your team members have to continuously monitor, process, and react to any information provided; you have to communicate with each other and with other parts of the sub. As long as communication is clear and unhindered, you can operate the sub safely. But when signals are distorted or transmissions clouded, you run the risk of serious damage to the sub and personal injury or harm to yourself or your crew.

Your brain is like the control room of a submarine. It's the command center of your body—not just your thought processes, but your bodily functions as well. The brain regulates your body temperature; it identifies sources of pain; it coordinates the movements of your arms and legs so you can walk, run, hit a ball, or clap your hands; it orchestrates your airflow and larynx so that you can talk, hum, or sing; it makes sense of visual images; it interprets sounds; it allows you to imagine and dream. To make these things happen, the brain processes information and communicates that information within itself and the rest of the body.

Communication in a submarine happens when voice or data signals travel over wires or wireless frequencies from the sender to the receiver. As the captain, you send a message by speaking into a microphone, which carries your voice electronically over communication wires to the person with whom you wish to communicate. In the

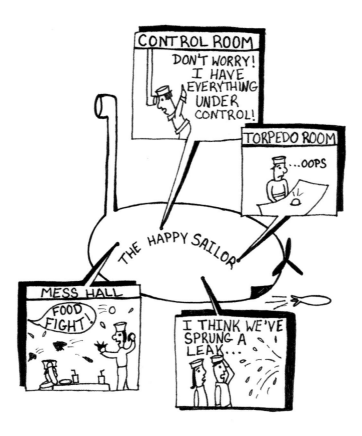

brain, instead of using wires or frequencies, nearly 100 billion brain cells called neurons carry the messages. Communication happens when the sending neuron, the presynaptic neuron, sends an electrical impulse down its long, thread-like limb, the axon, to the branches at the end of the limb, the dendrites. When the signal reaches the tip of the sending neuron's dendrites, it has to ride on special carrying chemicals called neurotransmitters over

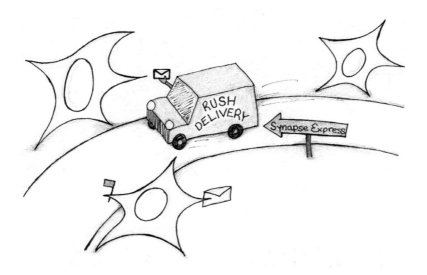

Communication between nerve cells.

the gap between that neuron and the others surrounding it (called the synapse) to the neuron whose job it is to receive the message, called the postsynaptic neuron.

This kind of communication between neurons is carried out literally billions of times per second to accomplish your bodily functions and thought processes, including everything from blowing your nose, to sleeping, to breathing, to reading a book, to having sexual impulses.

For our minds and bodies to work properly, however, communication between brain cells must stay in good working order. Inhaled or ingested chemical substances alter brain chemistry, especially of the neurotransmitters (how much the sending neuron releases to carry the signal, how much is accepted by the receiving neuron, and how much stays in the synapse), and when brain chemistry is altered, neuron communication is disrupted or breaks down. When communication between neurons breaks down, a person's thinking, feelings, and physical abilities change.

Most of us have seen someone who has had too much to drink, either in real life or on TV, and these characters share some typical behaviors: their speech may become slurred; they may fall down a lot; they may look hot or

Substance Abuse and Behavior

Because drug substances alter brain chemistry, they can cause users to do things they might not otherwise do:

- break promises
- neglect responsibilities
- blow off schoolwork
- start delinquent behaviors (lying, cheating, stealing, skipping school, etc.)
- run away from home
- have casual sex
- engage in prostitution
- commit crime
- vandalize property
- assault others
- commit rape
- try other, more dangerous drugs
- drive while high or drunk
- take dangerous physical risks

flushed; they may have difficulty walking or writing; they act stupid or say stupid things; they may become intensely emotional (angry, giddy, or sad); they may throw up; they may get sleepy or pass out. All of these behaviors are rooted in alcohol's affect on the neurotransmitters in the brain, especially a single type of neurotransmitter called GABA.

Alcohol, however, doesn't disrupt the GABA neurotransmitters of every part of the brain at the same time or rate, which is why you see a progression of various symptoms in a drunken person over time. To understand how alcohol and other chemical substances affect those who use them, we need to understand how different parts of the brain control different aspects of our bodies, minds, and emotions.

Parts of the Brain

The brain is an immensely complex organ, the intricacies of which we cannot explain fully in this chapter. Instead, we'll focus on those general areas of the brain most affected by substance use and abuse.

The Cerebrum

This is the largest and most important part of the brain; it controls higher thoughts and reasoning, memory, voluntary movement, sensory perception (site, sound, touch, etc.), speech, language, learning, and perception. The cerebrum is made up of four lobes, each controlling its own area of function: the frontal lobe, the parietal lobe, the occipital lobe, and the temporal lobe.

> ### The Cerebrum—A Place of Never-Ending Communication
>
> The cerebrum, made up of its four lobes, is divided into two halves called hemispheres. These halves are connected by a strong, saddle-shaped tissue called the corpus callosum. The corpus callosum alone contains more than 200 million axons carrying four billion message-carrying impulses per second between the two hemispheres!

THE CEREBELLUM

This part of the brain is located beneath the cerebrum at the back of the head. It controls automatic movement, involuntary posture, balance, and muscular coordination.

THE BRAIN STEM

This is the section below the cerebrum and in front of the cerebellum. All body signals must pass through here to move from the spinal cord to the brain. This part of the brain controls reflexes and involuntary actions.

Two additional areas within the lower brain are greatly impacted by chemical substances.

THE LIMBIC SYSTEM

This group of structures creates a person's emotional makeup, including pleasure and aggression.

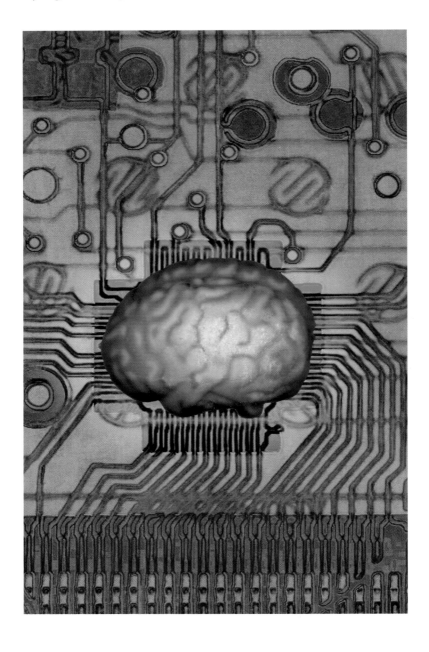

Types of Neurotransmitters in the Brain

Neurotransmitters are the chemical messengers that carry electrical impulses from one nerve cell, across the synapse (the space in between cells) to another nerve cell. Different types of messages require different types of neurotransmitters. These are just a few:

- seratonin
- dopamine
- GABA (gamma-aminobutyric acid)
- glycine
- acetylcholine
- epinephrine
- norepinephrine

Substance abuse can alter how much of these chemical messengers are produced, how they carry their messages, and whether or not they are able to deliver the message to the next cell. Different drug substances may affect different neurotransmitters, all of which are necessary for the brain's proper functioning.

THE HYPOTHALAMUS

This part of the limbic system balances overall body metabolism and regulates body temperature, emotions, hunger, thirst, and sleep patterns.

How a Substance Moves Through the Brain

We learned earlier in this chapter that chemical substances don't affect the same parts of the brain in the same way at the same time. Let's continue to use a person who has ingested too much alcohol to illustrate.

If that person drinks a shot of whiskey or downs a pint of beer, the beverage moves down the throat, into the stomach, and into the intestines, where the bulk of the beverage's alcohol content is absorbed into the bloodstream. (About 20 percent is absorbed into the blood while passing through the stomach; the rest is absorbed through the small intestine.) The blood then carries the alcohol throughout the body (liver, kidneys, brain, etc.). When alcohol reaches the brain, it first affects the cerebrum.

The "Reward" System

Some scientists call the limbic system the place of "reward." Why? Because whenever we experience pleasurable circumstances, the limbic system releases a specific kind of neurotransmitter called "dopamine," which creates pleasurable feelings. The more dopamine released, the more pleasure we feel. Most abused chemical substances affect the limbic system, creating a short-lasting feeling of pleasure called a "high."

How Chemical Substances Affect the Brain

Since the cerebrum regulates thinking, self-control, and the ability to process sight, sound, smell, and other senses, the drunken person might first become more carefree, less reserved, and more talkative. He may have difficulty seeing or hearing well, and may not notice minor bumps, scrapes, and bruises since he isn't processing pain sensations effectively. This person's ability to make good decisions, think clearly, or practice self-control may be seriously impaired. All this happens when alcohol reaches this first part of the brain.

Then the alcohol moves from the cerebrum into the limbic system. Since this set of structures controls emotional responses and memory, our drunk may become violently enraged or overwhelmingly sad. He may cry, throw things, or become aggressive. And he may not remember his behavior the next morning.

From the limbic system, the alcohol moves into the cerebellum, which controls and coordinates muscle movements and balance. Our intoxicated individual may become unsteady on his feet, lose his balance, or demonstrate stiff, jerky movements. This impact on the cerebellum is what police officers test for when they ask a suspected drunk driver to walk a straight line heel-to-toe or to touch her finger to her nose.

The alcohol continues its journey through the brain by next stopping at the hypothalamus (and the closely related pituitary gland, which controls hormone secretion). At this level of intoxication, the person may become sleepy or hungry, may need to urinate more, and may find his sexual desire has increased, although his ability to perform sexually is decreased.

Finally, the alcohol arrives at the brain stem, which controls all the survival functions your body performs of which you are usually unaware and over which you have little conscious control: breathing, body temperature

Exposing the Myths

MYTH: Drug addiction is the same thing as "a lot of" drug use.

FACT: Drug addiction and drug use are not degrees of the same thing. The original choice to use drugs is voluntary, and drug use can lead to addiction, but true addiction is never a choice. True addiction happens when drug substances alter the user's brain chemistry in such a way that the brain creates a chronic, compulsive, uncontrollable craving for the drug. Occasional drug users can quit when they want; addicts suffer from a drug-use-induced illness and cannot quit on their own.

regulation, heart rate, consciousness. A person with enough alcohol in the her blood to impact brain stem function can stop breathing, experience uncontrolled blood pressure, or develop an out-of-control rise in body temperature, all of which can be fatal.

Not Just the Brain!

If chemicals affected only the brain, that alone would be enough to cause serious damage, but these substances affect other parts of the body, too. How the drug is taken into the body impacts which additional parts of the body are affected.

Smoking, snorting, or inhaling will obviously irritate the nose, sinuses, airway, and lungs. Smokers develop coughs and get lung, mouth, and throat cancers. People

---

Am I a User or an Addict?

Every one of the following is a warning sign that drug use is becoming drug addiction. The more "yes" answers you have, the more likely it is that you have an addiction.

1. Do you get drunk or high regularly?
2. Do you think about or plan your substance use in advance?
3. Do you get drunk or high alone?
4. Is using making you sick or causing you ongoing physical symptoms?
5. Do you lie about how much or how often you are using?
6. Have you stopped doing things you used to enjoy so that you can get drunk or high?
7. Have your eating habits, sleep patterns, or mental abilities changed?
8. When you're not high, do you feel depressed, hopeless, run-down, or unmotivated?
9. Do you have blackouts or memory gaps?
10. Do you have to use more of the same substance to recapture your earlier highs?

Categories of Substance Abuse

EXPERIMENTAL USE: The person tries the substance once or twice.

RECREATIONAL USE: The person uses the substance socially, only when she is with friends or at a party.

CIRCUMSTANTIAL USE: The person uses the substance to escape or avoid the pain of personal problems or life circumstances. Or the person uses the substance to get him through a challenge or situation (takes caffeine-laced pills to stay awake to study, for example).

INTENSIFIED USE: The person's drug use increases over a long period. This is the regular user who experiences ongoing physical symptoms because of her drug use (sore throat, cough, runny nose, nosebleeds, weight loss, irritability, etc.).

COMPULSIVE USE: These are true addicts, who are prisoners of their drug use. They can no longer choose not to use and suffer significant life and health disruption because of their addiction.

who snort cocaine experience perpetual runny noses and chronic nosebleeds.

Substances that are ingested by swallowing, drinking, or eating (pills, liquids, laced food) irritate the linings of the stomach and intestines, can cause ulcers, and can increase blood flow to the stomach, which reduces blood flow to other parts of the body.

Virtually all chemical substances enter the bloodstream, not just those injected, so all are processed through the circulatory system (heart, lungs, veins, arteries, etc.) and pass through the body's most vital organs (including the pancreas and liver). This distribution throughout the vital organs explains liver disease in alcoholics and kidney failure in junkies.

In the next four chapters, we'll examine how different types of chemical substances impact the body in specific ways. We'll focus on the most commonly abused substances: gateway drugs (tobacco, alcohol, marijuana, and inhalants), medicines (steroids, over-the-counter drugs, and prescription medications), club drugs (Ecstasy, ketamine (Special K), and others), and other illegal drugs (narcotics, hallucinogens, and more).

3

DOORWAYS TO DANGER:
Tobacco, Alcohol, Marijuana, and Inhalants

One night. Five teens. A few beers. A bit of pot.

One Acura. One wooden telephone pole. One metal power pole. Lots of speed.

Three deaths. One serious injury. One set of minor injuries.

One trial. Three manslaughter convictions. Fifteen years.

The forty-one words you've just read summarize real-life events that began one carefree night in Tampa, Florida, in 1999.

Five teenagers—Michael Dale Jones, seventeen; Erin Kugler, eighteen; Ashley Rubera, fifteen; Jodee Suzanne Beam, nineteen; and Marc Berenguer, also nineteen— were hanging out, partying and having a good time together. Then Michael got a hold of his mother's black 1990 Honda Acura, and the five decided to head off to another party. It was 1:30 A.M.

Erin got in the front seat; Ashley, Jodee, and Marc climbed in the back. And almost immediately, the four teenage passengers knew they were in trouble.

Michael, who was legally drunk with a blood alcohol level of 0.12 and who had been smoking marijuana, apparently got a kick out of scaring his friends by swerving his car intentionally back and forth between lanes. When the teens begged and pleaded with him to stop, he angrily replied, "Don't tell me how to drive," then yanked the steering wheel even harder, causing the car to swerve again. Erin, who was sitting in the front seat, put on her seatbelt, fearing the worst might happen. It did.

Michael lost control of the car, which spun clockwise and then stuck a telephone pole and a utility pole. Two of the three passengers in the backseat, fifteen-year-old Ashley and nineteen-year-old Jodee, were thrown from the car and killed. The third rear-seat passenger, nineteen-year-old Marc, also died in the crash. Autopsies later revealed that all three victims had either alcohol or

Tobacco, Alcohol, Marijuana, and Inhalants

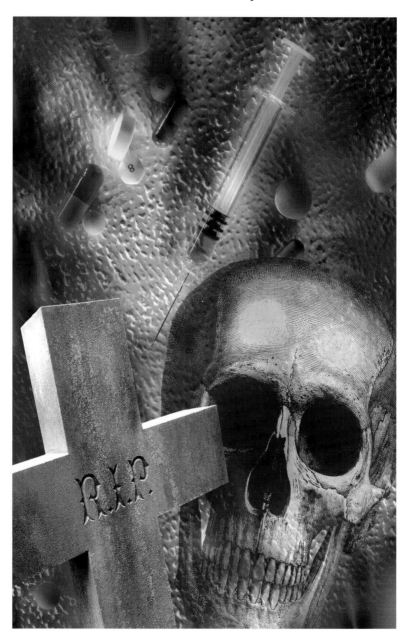

marijuana in their systems at the time of their deaths, just as the driver did.

The driver was knocked unconscious and taken to the intensive care unit. Erin, the only passenger to wear a seatbelt, was hospitalized briefly for minor injuries and released.

In April 2001, nineteen months after the accident, Michael Dale Jones was sentenced to fifteen years in prison for three counts of driving under the influence (DUI) manslaughter that cost the lives of his friends.

Four lives were destroyed that night, and a fifth permanently scarred. All for the sake of a high. What do you think? Was it worth it?

These five teens weren't doing anything that countless teens across North America don't do every weekend. They were doing what teens view as the "harmless" drugs: alcohol and marijuana. As some teens say, "It's not like they were doing crack!" They were just having a good time with some mild chemical enhancement, right?

All substance abuse is dangerous, even use of what teens view as milder drugs. The increased risk of death or injury by motor vehicle accident (MVA) alone is enough to make them dangerous, as the above story illustrates. The National Highway Traffic Safety Administration (NHTSA) reported that nearly one in three drivers ages fifteen to twenty who died in MVAs in 2002 had been drinking alcohol. Alcohol, or at least its effects, ultimately killed these teens.

But the increased likelihood of death or injury in an MVA isn't the only danger involved. We've already seen that all abused chemical substances affect the brain and body—drugs can make you sick, hurt your body, impair your ability to think or make decisions, or put you in an early grave. Even the "milder" drugs can do all this. But most teens already know about these dangers.

Perhaps the biggest danger of using the "milder" drugs is the tendency of teens to underestimate their power to cause harm and their propensity to open doors to harder drug use.

GATEWAY DRUGS

No teen wakes up one morning and decides, *Today, I'll become addicted to cocaine.* No twelve-year-old looks into his future and says, "What I really want to be when I grow up is a heroin addict." Something leads them there step by step.

When you attend a rock concert, for example, you make the choice to go. You choose which show to attend, you purchase the ticket, you arrange transportation, and you show up at the stadium where the concert is to be held. You don't just snap your fingers, and poof, you're there. Each step leads you closer to the live performance, but you're not there yet. In order to experience the thrill of the music in person you have to pass through the stadium gate. The gate is your way into a new level of music experience.

Similarly, tobacco, alcohol, marijuana, and inhalants function as the tickets and gate through which teen users pass to access a world of drugs they might never have been exposed to had they not tried these substances. These "gateway drugs" take the user a step further down the road of substance abuse. Unlike the concert-goer, the gateway drug user may not want to go where these drugs take him, but these drugs can put teens on an express train they just can't stop.

No Such Thing as "Minor" Drugs

Gateway drugs are every bit as serious as other drugs:

- They are just as illegal.
- They can be just as addictive.
- They can get you into just as much legal trouble.
- They can impair your abilities just as much as other drugs do.
- They can be just as harmful.
- They can kill.

The Center on Addiction and Substance Abuse at Columbia (CASA) found that adolescents between the ages of twelve and seventeen who used gateway drugs (defined for this study as tobacco, alcohol, and marijuana) were up to 266 times more likely to use cocaine than those who didn't use gateway drugs. Teens that used all three gateway drugs listed in this study were seventy-seven times more likely to use cocaine than those who used only one gateway drug. Using substances like cigarettes and beer ultimately led these teens to cocaine.

Gateway drugs don't have to lead teens to other drugs in order to bring harm to their users. These drugs, though viewed as mild by most teens, can be dangerous—even deadly—by themselves.

Tobacco, Alcohol, Marijuana, and Inhalants

Tobacco

"Hurry, hurry, hurry! Step right up, folks! Come this way!" the carnival hawker cries from his curtained platform. "This small white paper cylinder contains everything you need to turn your teeth brown, make your clothes stink, wrinkle your skin, rot your lungs, shorten your breath, rob you of energy, and give you cancer. Try some today! It will only cost you your life."

Sounds absurd, doesn't it? Yet, every statement in this fake advertisement can be true about tobacco products—cigarettes, bidis, cigars, pipe tobacco, chew. Each can do what's listed in the preceding paragraph. Do you ever hear these products advertised this way? Of course not. But as nineteenth-century circus entrepreneur P. T. Barnum used to say, "There's a sucker born every minute." And the tobacco companies know it.

How Do Gateway Drugs Promote Further Drug Use?

Gateway drugs lead teens to use other drugs two ways:

1. They affect thinking and judgment. If you're drunk, for example, you may find yourself saying yes to something you would never agree to if you were sober.
2. They break down inhibitions. Once you cross one moral boundary line, it becomes easier to cross the next.

Tobacco Facts

PRODUCT: tobacco (cigarettes, cigars, smokeless tobacco, etc.)

ADDICTIVE CHEMICAL/DRUG IN PRODUCT: nicotine

STREET NAMES: smokes, butts, cigs, chew, snuff, dip,
bidis, blunts (tobacco products laced with other chemicals)

DRUG FORM: rolled, wadded, caked, flavored

HOW TAKEN: smoked, chewed, wadded in mouth, sniffed

HOW IT WORKS: causes neurons to release unusually
large amounts of the neurotransmitter dopamine, which
stimulates the brain's pleasure and reward center

EFFECTS: increases heart rate, blood pressure, and
breathing rate, causes more blood sugar to be released
into the blood, gives users feelings of energy, increased
mental alertness, pleasure, reduced appetite, and weight
loss

HEALTH HAZARDS: rapid addiction, reduced stamina for
exercise and sports, dulled senses of taste and smell,
chronic cough, shortness of breath, gum disease, tooth
loss, chronic lung disease, heart disease, stroke, mouth
and throat cancers, other cancers, pregnancy complica-
tions, skin damage

What's Really in a Cigarette?

- dead frog preservative (formaldehyde)
- rat poison chemicals (cyanide)
- insecticide (nicotine)

Despite the widespread education of young people about the dangers of tobacco, and despite the fact that tobacco products are illegal for those under eighteen years old, more than 3,000 teens in the United States become new regular smokers each day. According to the Centers for Disease Control and Prevention (CDC), tobacco use snares more than one million new users each year. Why? Because a chemical in tobacco called nicotine, a highly addictive substance, gives smokers a "kick" in a very short amount of time.

After someone inhales tobacco smoke, it takes only eight seconds for nicotine to reach the brain, causing an almost immediate sense of pleasure. But in less than forty minutes, more than half of the nicotine's effects are gone, so the user wants to light up again to get more of the drug. Her body has the desire. In a very short time, the user's brain is so altered that she becomes addicted.

According to the American Academy of Pediatrics, tobacco products are one of the first drug substances

Young People and Tobacco

Of all young people under eighteen years of age who are alive today, more than five million will die early deaths from a smoking-related disease (CDC).

> ### Cigarettes and Cancer
>
> - Cigarette smoking causes 90 percent of all lung cancer cases.
> - Cancer deaths (all kinds) are twice as high among smokers than nonsmokers.
> - Heavy smokers are four times more likely to die from cancer (all kinds) as nonsmokers.

young people try. This makes the decision to use or not use tobacco especially important. The decision about this drug may impact every other decision about drug substances. The decision to use or not use the next gateway drug, alcohol, has the same power to influence future drug use decisions.

ALCOHOL

Just because alcohol is legal for those over twenty-one years of age does not mean that it is more "safe" or less harmful than other drug substances. The Palo Alto Medical Foundation found that on college campuses all over the United States, alcohol abuse was involved in about two-thirds of all violent behavior, nearly half of all physical injuries, about one-third of all emotional difficulties, and almost 30 percent of all academic problems. A study done by the Nemours Foundation found that teens who drank alcohol regularly were more likely to have problems in school, to try other drugs, and to participate in delinquent behaviors such as stealing or vandalism. This study also followed these teens into adulthood and discovered that even as adults they had more difficulty getting and keeping jobs, maintaining healthy relationships, had higher incidences of addiction and substance abuse, and were more likely to be involved in criminal and violent behavior.

These risks are nothing new to kids today; twenty-first-century teens are well informed of alcohol-related statistics. They know all about the dangers of drinking and driving and the risks of getting drunk and having sex. They are fully aware that alcohol and its effects can de-

61

Drowning in Alcohol?

The CDC estimates that 40 percent of adolescent drowning accidents involve alcohol.

stroy people's lives. But their knowledge doesn't keep them from drinking.

Columbia University's National Center on Addiction and Substance Abuse found that more than five million high school students binge drink at least once a month, despite the fact that 77 percent of these students stated that they'd had at least one serious problem related to their drinking in the past year. Another study done by the same university found that more than 67 percent (or two

Alcohol Facts

ADDICTIVE CHEMICAL/DRUG IN PRODUCT: ethyl alcohol, (ethanol)

STREET NAME(S): brew, booze, juice, brewskies, hooch, sauce, cold ones

DRUG FORM: clear liquid that is diluted or blended to make beer, wine, wine coolers, liquor (gin, scotch, etc.), liqueur, alcopops ("Hard Lemonade," "Hooper's Hooch," "Sublime," "Spiked Lemonade," etc.)

HOW TAKEN: swallowed in drinks (can be blended with nonalcoholic beverages, juices, or fruits)

HOW IT WORKS: slows down the brain's ability to respond and communicate, and depresses the central nervous system

EFFECTS: initial feeling of relaxation, sociability, giddiness, or happiness, which can turn to depression, anger, sleepiness, confusion, and loss of self-control

HEALTH HAZARDS: risk of addiction, dizziness, nausea, vomiting, blackouts, memory loss, passing out in unsafe situation or places, decreased self-control and inhibitions, decreased sexual ability, diminished ability to feel pain, day after hangover effect (headache, nausea, fatigue, dry mouth, sore muscles, lethargy), injury or death related to alcohol impairment (motor vehicle accidents, falls, drowning, etc.), acute alcohol poisoning, chronic liver disease, heart disease, pancreatitis, ulcers, death by nervous system failure or choking (on own vomit while unconscious)

Hidden Dangers of Using Alcohol

- risk of addiction
- health risks when mixed with other abused drugs
- health risks when mixed with medications
- increased risk of accident, injury, or death when combined with driving
- increased risk of problems at home, school, work, or with friends
- increased risk of unwanted sexual encounters
- risk of long-term disease
- risk of death from alcohol poisoning

out of three) of young people who started drinking before the age of fifteen would later try an illegal drug like marijuana, heroin, or cocaine. Alcohol, like nicotine, is a gateway to later use of other drugs.

What Is a Standard Drink?

Each of these contains about the same amount of alcohol:

- one twelve-ounce bottle of beer
- one twelve-ounce wine cooler
- one five-ounce glass of wine
- one and a half ounces of 80-proof liquor

A beer, a glass of wine, and a shot glass of hard liquor contain about the same amounts of alcohol.

Facts About Inhalants

ADDICTIVE CHEMICAL/DRUG IN PRODUCT: various chemical vapors

STREET NAMES: amys, bang, bolt, gluey, head cleaner, hippie crack, kick, moon gas, poor man's pot, poppers, snappers, whippets

DRUG FORM: various household substances including solvents (paint thinners, spot removers, correction fluids, glues, rubber cement, gasoline, felt-tip markers, etc.), aerosols (spray deodorants, spray paint, hair products, cooking products, fabric protectors, etc.), gases (ether, chloroform, "laughing gas," which is nitrous oxide), and nitrites (room deodorizers, capsules that are "popped" or "snapped")

HOW TAKEN: "huffed" (inhaled deeply) directly from containers or from cloth soaked in the substance, sprayed directly into the nose or mouth, poured onto clothing and inhaled from cuffs or sleeves, sprayed into plastic or paper bags and inhaled (called "bagging"), inhaled from balloons

HOW IT WORKS: dilates blood vessels and produces high levels of toxins in the blood

EFFECTS: a short-lasting, quick high with strong hallucinations, delusions, feelings of weightlessness, increased sexual enhancement, and reduced inhibition

HEALTH HAZARDS: addiction, dizziness, short-term memory loss, hearing loss, slurred speech, impaired judgment, weight loss, muscle weakness, distractibility, loss of coordination, irritability, seizures, damage to the user's major organs, and possibility of death

One reason teens still choose to use alcohol is their tendency to underestimate its dangers and overestimate their ability to handle its effects.

The severity of alcohol's effects on the body depends on how much alcohol is used, the body weight and size of the individual who is drinking, how much food is in his stomach, and how quickly the alcohol is consumed. Generally, it takes only one or two standard drinks to make a teen begin to feel the effects of alcohol.

Inhalants

Eleven-year-old Chantelle didn't want to keep going to after-school care at the youth center. She was bored with routine and thought she was old enough to hang out at home by herself. Her single working mother felt differently.

Well, if I can't go home after school, the six-grader thought, *I may as well have some fun.*

The next day, with a recently purchased can of air freshener tucked safely in her deep coat pocket, Chantelle went happily to after-school care. Ducking into the girl's bathroom, she pulled out the aerosol can and sprayed air freshener all over the sleeves of her sweater. Then she quietly went back to a table at the far side of the center's cafeteria, sat down, put her coat over her head, and rested her head on her folded arms. Her soaked sleeves reeked of air freshener fumes within the cocoon she'd make for herself underneath her jacket. She soon felt the rush of lightheadedness and euphoria she expected, but no one else noticed. Chantelle never anticipated that the fumes that made her feel so good would nearly kill her.

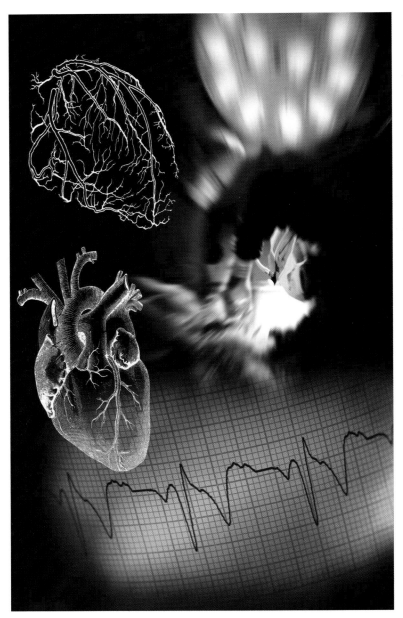

Inhaling chemical vapors can have a dangerous effect on heart function.

An Endless Supply

More than 1,000 common household products can be used as inhalants, and every one of them has the potential to kill.

(Partnership for a Drug-Free America)

Staff workers, who thought the young girl was sleeping, realized something was terribly wrong when Chantelle fell out of her seat and began convulsing on the floor. Only the quick-thinking action of the youth center staff and near-immediate response of paramedics to the center's 911 call saved the girl's life. "Huffing" had proved to be not the good time she had anticipated.

"Huffing," "bagging," and "sniffing" are all terms referring to the process of inhaling chemical vapors in order to get high. The chemicals used for huffing are called inhalants. The U.S. Department of Justice estimates that inhalants are the fourth most commonly abused substances by teenagers, following only alcohol, cigarettes, and marijuana. Because most substances used for huffing are common household products, adolescents have easy access to an unlimited supply. Most teens don't realize that huffing can kill them the first time it's tried.

"A person high on inhalants can feel playful one minute and in two minutes be dead."

—Earl Seigal, Director of the Drug and Poison Information Center in Cincinnati, Ohio

It's the most-used illegal drug in the United States, used by more than 11 million people annually, and by more than 71 million people over their lifetimes. It is the third-most abused substance by teenagers. It can be easier to obtain than alcohol. It's made from a plant that contains more than four hundred different chemicals, and it produces another two thousand chemicals when burned. Some people say it's a medicinal drug and should be legalized; others say it's a dangerous, highly addictive hallucinogen. Despite its apparent popularity, the National Institute on Drug Abuse (NIDA) maintains that marijuana, though widely used among adults, is not common among teens. According to NIDA, fewer than one in four high school seniors and fewer than one in five tenth-graders currently use marijuana.

> One marijuana joint contains the same amount of cancer-causing chemicals as twenty cigarettes!

Those who do smoke marijuana tell of a wide range of experiences when they get high. Some feel calm and relaxed; some feel very little of anything at all; others get extreme cravings for food (the "munchies"); still others experience bad highs where all they feel is fear, anxiety, and ***paranoia***. Virtually all users tell of how quickly the drug takes effect, but few realize how long marijuana lingers in the body after the high wears off.

After it has been smoked, marijuana reaches the brain within seconds and can affect the user's brain for four to

70

Marijuana Facts

ADDICTIVE CHEMICAL/DRUG IN PRODUCT: THC (delta-9-tetrahydrocannabinol)

STREET NAME(S): dope, grass, pot, herb, joints, Mary Jane, reefer, ganja, skunk, weed, blunt, gangster, chronic (there are more than 200 slang terms for marijuana)

DRUG FORM: dried shredded or crumbled leaves rolled into cigarettes, smoked in pipes, bongs, or hollowed-out cigars called "blunts," mixed into foods, or brewed as tea

HOW TAKEN: usually smoked as a cigarette (called a joint or nail), smoked in a pipe, bong, or blunt, or swallowed in food or tea

HOW IT WORKS: goes to the brain via the bloodstream, then to the rest of the body. Once in the brain, it coats or thickens brain cells, which slows down communication between cells.

EFFECTS: increases heart rate, slows thinking, slows reaction time, gives feelings of euphoria, contentment, relaxation, confusion, impaired balance and coordination, and paranoia

HEALTH HAZARDS: physically and psychologically addictive, causes respiratory infections, chronic cough, bronchitis, emphysema, compromised immune system, *panic attacks*, paranoia, a need for increased usage for same effect, impaired memory, learning difficulties, increased heart rate, anxiety, and is a gateway to harder drugs

Dying for Acceptance

Choose carefully which doors you open—and which you choose to leave shut.

six hours—a typical high. Though the effects of marijuana wear off in these few hours, traces of marijuana can be found in users' blood for days afterward. It's a highly traceable drug, accounting for many teens' failures to pass a drug test (for sports or jobs).

WHERE DO WE GO FROM HERE?

We've looked at the facts about the four most popular gateway drugs. We've seen why and how they are used and examined their potential health risks. Only you can decide if these are risks you're willing to take. As you weigh your decision, however, remember that gateway drugs have the strong potential to lead to other drug substances. The remaining chapters of this book will provide the information you need to make an informed decision about their use.

4

HELPFUL DRUGS, HURTFUL HIGHS:
Steroids, OTCs, and Prescription Drugs

His teachers called him "busy." His friends say he was "annoying." His grandmother said he was "spirited." But all Ryan knew was that it was hard to concentrate, difficult to control his emotions, and nearly impossible to sit still. His doctors said he had attention-deficit/hyperactivity disorder (ADHD) and prescribed the drug methylphenidate, which goes by the trade name Ritalin®. It proved to be a miracle drug for the eleven-year-old. Ryan's thinking cleared, he could concentrate, and he wasn't nearly as distracted. For once he felt calm and focused. He liked the feeling.

Ryan liked the feeling so much, that by the time he was thirteen years old, he was crushing his Ritalin tablets and snorting them.

Maria felt really lousy with the flu, but her working parents had job responsibilities and couldn't stay home from work to care for their fourteen-year-old daughter. Not knowing what else to do, the teen rooted through the family medicine cabinet and found some Coricidin HBP Maximum Strength Flu® tablets that contained dextromethorphan (DXM). She tried taking the recommended two fifteen-milligram tablet dose, but an hour later was still coughing so hard she thought she might not catch her breath. Thinking, *If some helps a little, then more must help a lot*, Maria downed eight more of the round red pills. In just a short time, Maria felt like she was outside of her body, dissociated from the flu, and experiencing wonderful hallucinations. Unknown to the high-school freshman, she was experiencing a high on what some of her peers would call skittles, red devils, or Triple C. When the high wore off, she couldn't wait to take more.

Everyone thought Charles would make the final cut for the wrestling team. Small, quick, and very coordinated, the high-school sophomore was a shoo-in for the 110-pound weight class. That is, until the new kid showed up for pre-season workouts. Poised, muscular, and clearly

Males who want to achieve a certain body type, whether for sports or appearance, may be tempted to take steroids.

stronger than Charles, the fifteen-year-old had more muscle definition in his arms than Charles had in his entire body. Charles didn't stand a chance.

On his way out of practice, an upperclassman offered him some "gym candy," anabolic steroids the older wrestler assured Charles would help him bulk up fast and gain more strength. Charles jumped at the chance. In just four weeks' time, he felt like a new wrestler: stronger and more toned. At tryouts, he pinned the new kid in just twenty-five seconds into their first round of competition and won the spot on the wrestling team. Everything seemed to be going great, until purple and red spots erupted all over his body.

After the car accident, Naomi's doctors put her on Percocet®, a pain reliever, for the severe headaches and neck and back pain she experienced as a result of her concussion and whiplash. When that pain reliever didn't seem

---

Street Names for Commonly Abused Medicines

- Steroids: Arnolds, gym candy, juice, pumpers, stackers, weight trainers
- Ritalin®: kibbles and bits, kiddy cocaine, skippy, smarties, vitamin R, pineapple
- Coricidin HBP Cough & Cold Medicine®: Triple C, CCC, candy, skittles, red devils
- Other cough and cold medicines containing dextromethorphan: DXM, dex, robo, skittles, velvet
- OxyContin®: Oxy, OC, oxycotton, killers

> ### Not Always Addictive
>
> According to the U.S. National Institute on Drug Abuse, addiction to pain relievers, stimulants, tranquilizers, and sedatives rarely occurs if the drugs are taken as instructed by a physician.

to work as well as expected, physicians switched the sixteen-year-old to OxyContin®, another pain reliever.

While at school one afternoon several weeks into her treatment, Naomi happened to mention to another student that she was taking Oxy for pain.

"Have you ever sucked the coating off the tablet when you took it?" her friend asked.

"No," Naomi replied. "Why would I?"

"Because it makes more of the drug go into your system sooner; you'll get better relief from your pain."

When she got home that evening, Naomi tried what her friend had suggested, thinking she would find faster pain relief. She experienced pain relief all right, along with an incredible rush of euphoria and feelings of well-being. After one experience with an Oxy high, the teenager was hooked.

What do Ryan, Maria, Charles, and Naomi have in common? They all used potentially good, legal medicines in an unhealthy, illegal way. Ryan's Ritalin was a prescription drug used to treat his ADHD. Maria's flu medicine was a common formula anyone can purchase off the shelf at a drug store, grocery, or pharmacy that is used to treat common cold or flu symptoms. Charles' steroids were legal substances available by prescription only used to treat things like muscle inflammation, delayed *pu-*

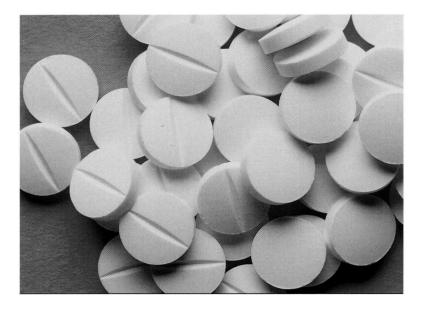

Legal medicines can be addictive and destructive when taken improperly.

berty, or muscle wasting in people with **chronic** diseases. Naomi's medication was legitimately prescribed by her doctor to treat postaccident pain, but her new means of taking the drug pushed her into becoming addicted.

These drug substances were designed to treat specific medical conditions; they were never meant to be abused. But like all chemical substances, these drugs have the potential to alter a person's mental or physical state. And because many of these medicines are so widely available in North America, they've become a cheap, easy high for teenagers.

The National Drug Intelligence Center (NDIC) estimates that one in ten teens between the ages of twelve and seventeen have used these kinds of medicines in a nonmedical way. In other words, they've used them to get high. Another government institution, SAMHSA, estimates that over five million teens and young adults used prescription medications illegally in 2001. And that number, according to SAMHSA, is rising.

In identifying which prescription medications teens abuse most, the Partnership for a Drug Free America divides these medications into four general categories: pain relievers (also called analgesics), tranquilizers, stimulants, and sedatives.

Pain Relievers

Naomi's Percocet and OxyContin were both prescription pain relievers. Sometimes called analgesics, these drugs usually fall into a class of drugs called opioids (which come from opium) and are considered narcotics. As this category name implies, doctors prescribe these medicines to ease pain. For severe pain, physicians may prescribe morphine, Percocet, OxyContin, or Darvon. For milder pain, many will prescribe codeine.

These drugs work so well in treating pain because they prevent pain messages from being received in the brain

> ### Did You Know?
>
> Prescription painkillers and the illegal drug substance known as heroin come from the same plant source (poppies). Their ingredients are very similar.

Once Might Be Enough

A single overdose of pain relievers like OxyContin can cause death from respiratory depression.

by blocking pain receptors. Like all abused substances, pain relievers alter brain chemistry in such a way that the brain not only doesn't receive pain messages, but that

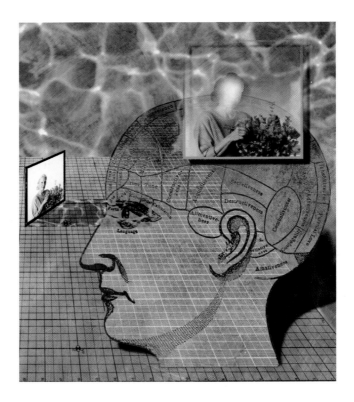

Medications are powerful chemicals that can have unpredictable effects on the human brain.

the pleasure center is stimulated. When abused, these drugs can produce a great sense of well-being, pleasure, and euphoria.

What Naomi soon realized was that she needed more and more Oxy to repeat her highs. Most pain relievers work so that the body builds up a tolerance for them; in other words, the body requires more and more of the drug to get the desired effect. This can lead to physical dependence and chemical addiction. When taken at high doses, these kinds of drugs can slow breathing rate so much that it stops all together. Abusing pain relievers can kill you. Yet painkillers are the prescription drugs most widely abused by teenagers.

Tranquilizers

You've probably seen a movie in which doctors gave a hysterical woman or psychotic man some kind of medication to calm him or her down. Some of these drugs are called tranquilizers. Valium®, Xanax®, Halcion®, Librium®, and Prosom® are brand-name tranquilizers that fall into the chemical family called benzodiazepines. These drugs work on the GABA neurotransmitters in the

> ### Legal Doesn't Mean Safe
>
> Prescription and OTC medications, when not taken according to a doctor's advice, are every bit as dangerous as illegal drugs or alcohol.

brain, slowing down brain communication and activity. Because these drugs tend to have a calming effect, they are often prescribed for things like anxiety or panic attacks, tension, stress, and sleep disorders.

When taken as prescribed, they can make a person feel sleepy, calm, or peaceful. But when taken at higher doses than doctors recommend, they can create addictions, cause seizures, suppress breathing, and slow your heart rate. Extreme overdoses or mixing these medicines with other drugs or alcohol can kill you.

Stimulants

If tranquilizers slow you down, stimulants speed you up. This group of substances increases brain communication and activity by increasing the amount of the neurotransmitter dopamine in the brain, which causes greater alertness, an increased ability to concentrate, a better attention span, and more energy. This effect is exactly what Ryan needed to help him with his ADHD. Ritalin (methylphenidate), the drug Ryan used, and Dexedrine® (dextroamphetamine) are the two stimulants teens abuse most.

> ### Don't Forget
> ### About Interactions
>
> Mixing medicines with other drugs, illicit substances, or alcohol can kill you.

> ### Other Considerations
>
> Teens who abuse cough and cold medications don't just put themselves at risk of DXM overdose. Most OTC cough and cold products contain other chemicals that are equally dangerous if taken in high doses.

When stimulants are taken too often or in too high a dose, they can cause blood pressure to skyrocket, heart and respiration rates to increase, and the body temperature to rise to dangerously high levels. They can also cause feelings of hostility and paranoia. Heart attacks and fatal seizures are common at high doses.

SEDATIVES

Nembutal® and Mebaral® are two common sedatives many teens have heard of. Like tranquilizers, sedatives slow the body down, but unlike tranquilizers sedatives come from a chemical family called barbiturates. Because sedatives slow down the entire central nervous system, they are sometimes called "sleeping pills."

The effect sedatives have on their users is similar to the effect caused by tranquilizers; they produce a calming effect or drowsiness by slowing respiration rate and acting on the brain's GABA neurotransmitter. Doctors prescribe sedatives to help patients sleep or to relieve tension or, in some cases, to make a person who is having a seizure stop convulsing.

> ### A Pill Is Not Always What It Seems
>
> Many medications can look very similar: same size tablet, pill, or capsule, same color, same form. But drugs vary in potency (how much of the drug is actually in the pill). Four pills of one substance might have only a mild effect, while four similar-looking pills of another substance might be lethal.

Like tranquilizers, too much of these drugs can kill you, and mixing these drugs with alcohol can be fatal.

Not Just Prescriptions

As we saw with Maria in this chapter's opening illustrations, prescription drugs are not the only medicines teens can abuse. OTCs like cough and cold medicines or diet formulas can be abused as well. OTCs are perfectly legal drug substances that any teenager can buy wherever these drugs are sold. The most commonly abused OTC is any cough, cold, or flu medicine containing the chemical dextromethorphan (DXM). DXM is a cough suppressant, and when taken at higher-than-recommended doses, it can cause hallucinations and feelings of detachment from your surroundings.

Usually taken as capsules, gel caps, tablets, or syrup, DXM can cause a long-lasting high. Teens who take high doses can be under the influence of this drug for six hours or more. Because their thinking and judgment are impaired for so long, these teens run great risk of injury.

DXM is safe and nonaddictive when taken as directed on the package label, but when abused, DXM can cause exceptionally high fevers, vomiting, irregular heartbeat, high blood pressure, headache, numbness, loss of consciousness, seizures, brain damage, and death.

So How Much Is Enough?

A normal recommended does of DXM to ease cough and cold symptoms is 15 to 30 mg every four to six hours. Teens who use DXM to get high take, on average, more than 360 mg in a single dose. That's anywhere from roughly ten to twenty times the recommended dosing guidelines.

The most widely abused cough suppressant medicine that contains DXM is a product called Coricidin HBP Cough and Cold. Often called Triple C, this medication is taken by mouth and causes the same symptoms listed for DXM products. It is especially popular at all-night dance parties called raves.

How to Protect Yourself
from Date Rape Drugs

If you choose to party at raves or other social gatherings, there are a few simple steps you can take to protect yourself from date rape drugs:

- Never accept an open beverage from any-one, not even those you know.
- Only accept a beverage if it is sealed in its original container, or if you can watch it be opened and poured.
- Never leave your drink unattended.

hypnol, because of their tendencies to cause amnesia. If the victim can't remember the assault, she can't press charges against the perpetrator.

Date rape is the most common form of rape (forced or coerced sex), with one in four girls, or 25 percent, expected to become victims of rape before they reach age twenty-five. Three out of five rapes occur before a woman turns eighteen. Aside from what club drugs can

Ecstasy—A Drug of Youth

Eighty percent of Ecstasy-related emergency room visits involve people age twenty-five years and younger.

—(*USA Today*, citing a Drug Abuse Warning Network report).

do to your body, one of the greatest threats club drugs pose is their ability to make rave-goers vulnerable to sexual assault or compromised sexual choices.

Unlike many other drug substances, several club drugs serve absolutely no medical purpose. In the United States, Ecstasy is classified as a Schedule 1 substance under the Controlled Substances Act, meaning that it has a high likelihood of being abused and that it has no legitimate medical purpose. In Canada, Ecstasy is considered a Class H substance under the Food and Drug Act, meaning that there is no known medical use for the drug and that its use is illegal in all circumstances. It is illegal in both countries to buy, sell, or possess club drugs.

Buyer Beware

Another danger of club drugs of which most teens are unaware is the inconsistency between batches of the very same drug. Because many club drugs are home-made, it's impossible to know how much of any one substance is in a pill, a capsule, or a blunt. Two E pills on one night might barely affect you; two from another seller on a different night could be fatal.

That's what happened to sixteen-year-old Brandy French. The healthy honors' student who'd never tried Ecstasy before attended a day-long concert in May 2001 with some friends who introduced her to E. After taking one half of an E pill, Brandy seemed to be okay. Four hours later, she took the other half of the pill and began to feel sick. Her friends didn't seek medical help. She slipped into unconsciousness and died later that

How can I tell if a friend is using club drugs?

The National Clearinghouse for Alcohol and Drug Information suggests that you look for these symptoms:

- short-term memory problems
- dizziness
- fainting
- loss of physical coordination
- confusion
- depression
- sleep problems
- chills
- sweats

evening. Brandy's total dose of Ecstasy was only one pill, split over four hours.

Club drugs are dangerous drugs, just like any other abused substances. As you weigh their benefits with their potential hazards, do you really think they are worth trying? Think about what it might cost you. Then decide.

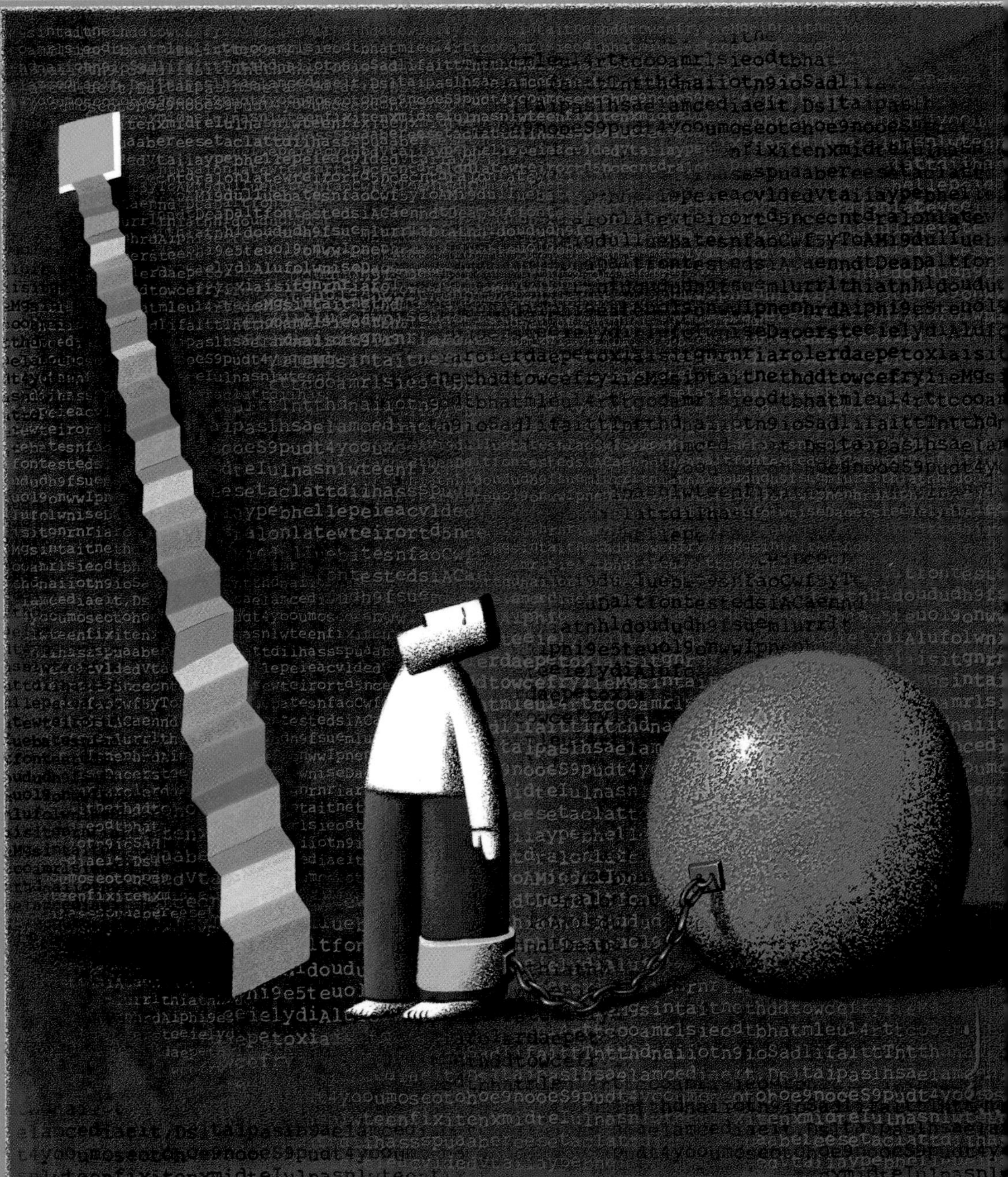

6

HEROIN, HOPE, AND HANGING IN THERE

*D*ear Prospective Teen User,

I've been where you are right now. I've walked in your shoes. I know what it's like to be so angry with everything and everybody that you just don't care anymore. I've wanted to escape my parents' bickering and my teachers' nagging. I've been tempted to drown my heartache in a sea of mind-numbing booze. I've even been just plain old bored with nothing better to do, and curiosity got the best of me. Believe me, I've been there, which is why I'm writing to you.

If I could say just three words to you it would be, "Don't do it!" If I could say just four more, it would be, "It's not worth it." How do I know? I'm a sixteen-year-old addict. Let me tell you what you have in store for you if you decide to pursue this game.

At first, it might feel like a thrill. You know, like the first time you lie or cheat on a test. You might get a knot in your

Drug use can make it difficult for your body to sleep normally.

stomach and feel a little nervous, but that will wear off. Once you cross the first line into using, the next line gets easier to cross.

You'll begin to realize soon enough that nothing is going to recapture the thrill of that first high: more drugs, higher doses, different substances—none of them will repeat your first experience. Oh, you'll look for it, and you'll think you're mastering your substance of choice, but the truth is, it will master you.

It will take over your thinking. It will take over your time. It will take over your money, friendships, work, and school life. It will consume you (more like chew you up and spit you out). The rush of the high won't last as long, and it will tease you into wanting more. Then you'll be trapped, like you swore would never happen.

Your druggie friends, who were so nice to you when they got you started on their drugs, will start asking you to pay up—no more freebies. If you can't pay, they may require "favors." That might mean sex you never imagined you'd do in this lifetime.

You'll start having trouble sleeping soon enough, you may feel lousy, and you may start having memory trouble. Anything you cared about before will fade in comparison to your new first love: substance abuse is a jealous lover; it won't compete with anything else. When you can't get enough, you'll fall into depression and despair. Then the voices of suicide will haunt you. If you get desperate enough, you may even decide to quit, but by then, you'll be physically tied to the drug. Quitting won't be easy; it will make you sick at first. And everything in you will pant for a taste of that once-sweet high. You may make it, with help, or you may not. Who knows?

You see, the only sure way to avoid addiction is to never start using at all. If only someone had told me.

Dying for Acceptance

But someone is telling you. That someone is me. Don't do it. Think about what it could mean to you, your family, your friends, your future. Is the cheap thrill of a moment really worth your life?

Maybe my mistakes can be a lesson for you. Take it from me. I've been there and am paying the cost for my choice. But if my suffering can help you, then maybe it's at least worth something. I sure hope so. I don't want it to have all been a waste.

Hang in there.
Jamie, 16
resident at a heroin rehab facility

We looked at several drug substances in this book so far, and we've focused on those most likely to be used by teens. But one more drug, a very deadly one, has resurged in popularity in recent years. And it's one that will take over your life every bit as much as it did Jamie's: heroin.

A Growing Problem

Most teens know that heroin, like cocaine, is a dangerous drug that should be avoided, but as the price of heroin declined to only $10 a dose, its use soared among teens. From 1990 to 1996, heroin use among twelfth-graders in the United States doubled. By 1999, according to NIDA's MTF study, the rates for heroin use had nearly tripled those of 1991. The average age of first-time heroin users fell from nearly twenty-seven years old in 1991 to just under eighteen years old by 1997. New heroin users are no longer adults; now they are teens.

Heroin, Hope, and Hanging In There

The 2002 National Survey on Drug Use and Health revealed that roughly 3.7 million Americans age twelve and older had tried heroin at least once in their lifetimes. Nearly 30 percent of twelfth-graders said heroin was easy to obtain. Heroin, some said, was even easier to obtain than marijuana or alcohol!

Why all the fuss? Heroin is *highly* addictive and can ensnare users after only one dose. It also carries a host of other high-risk issues. To understand the risks, we have to understand what heroin is and how it works.

The Hubbub on Heroin

STREET NAMES FOR HEROIN:	smack, horse, big H, black tar, gumball, tootsie roll, H, junk, Harry, scag, sugar, powder
HOW HEROIN IS USED:	Injected into a vein or muscle, smoked, inhaled through a straw, or snorted
WHAT IT FEELS LIKE:	Immediate intense pleasure, a "rush" of euphoria
IMMEDIATE EFFECTS	Flushing of face and skin, dry mouth, heavy limbs, drowsiness, clouded thinking
DANGERS	Powerful, near-immediate addiction, collapsed veins, abscesses, liver disease, pneumonia, hepatitis risk, HIV risk, heart infections, severe depression, risk of overdose, death

Many don't *want* to because the high still means too much to them. Some, like Jamie, will realize that the cost isn't worth it, and when they get to that point, they're ready to try to change.

Giving up heroin, however, can be dangerous, especially if attempted

> ### Killer Heroin
>
> Medical examiners report that heroin is one of the top three most frequently reported causes of drug-abuse deaths.

without medical help. Because users' bodies have grown so accustomed to heroin in their systems, they experience something called withdrawal, where their bodies, especially their brains, have to learn to live without the powerful drug. According to NIDA, symptoms of heroin withdrawal can be severe: extreme drug craving, restlessness, muscle pain, bone pain, inability to sleep, diarrhea, vomiting, cold flashes, thrashing, kicking, and convulsions. Withdrawal symptoms reach their peak two or three days after quitting and, for most people, continue for about a week. For some, symptoms can last for months.

Seeing the dangers of heroin outlined here and learning how difficult it is for an addict to quit might make you think that Jamie, the sixteen-year-old author whose letter begins this chapter, has little hope of recovery. Not so, say the researchers at NIDA. There are many more treatment options for addicts today than there were in ages past: ***behavioral therapies***, group support systems, hospital programs, home-based programs, medications to ease withdrawal symptoms, life-skill training opportunities, psychiatric support, ***methadone*** clinics, and religious-based initiatives. With the appropriate medical help— and getting medical help is the key—even the most ad-

Dying for Acceptance

Addiction is a dangerous disease—but there are ways out.

Famous People Killed by Heroin

- John Belushi, comedian
- Janis Joplin, singer
- Chris Farley, comedic actor
- Layne Staley, singer
- Kristen Pfaff, bassist
- River Phoenix, actor

dicted person can successfully stop using heroin and return to a more stable, productive life. But he will need help, and he needs to want to be helped. And he has to be willing to be helped in several areas of his life.

Addiction is a complex disease, regardless of the substance involved, so it has the potential to disrupt every part of a user's life. Treatment options therefore need to address a broad spectrum of issues, not just the medical component: family relationships, friendships, jobs, housing, schooling, other health issues, mental health, nutrition, and more. It's a process that will take time. Some programs take ninety days, others take twelve months, still others may need addiction treatment for a

Funny Phrase Origins

The terms "kick the habit" and going "cold turkey" come from heroin withdrawal symptoms. When heroin users stop using heroin, they can experience cold flashes marked by goose bumps ("cold turkey") and jerking leg movements they can't control ("kick the habit").

Dying for Acceptance

A person with an addiction may seem like two different people—and it may be difficult to tell which is the real person.

period of years. Because Jamie is young, his likelihood of successful treatment is greater than someone who'd been abusing drugs for decades. There is simply less change in his brain chemistry to undo.

Helping Someone You Love

Maybe you know someone like Jamie. Maybe you've watched a family member or good friend struggle with addiction. It might not be to heroin; it could be to any chemical substance that will give them a high. Maybe you only suspect a friend is using. Is there anything you can do?

Emergency Symptoms

If you or a friend suffers any of the following while using chemical substances, get medical help immediately:

- loss of consciousness
- inability to be wakened
- prolonged or violent vomiting
- vomiting blood
- convulsions
- seizures
- severe abdominal pain
- nonresponsiveness
- uncontrolled fever

Dying for Acceptance

First, be sure about your suspicions. In chapter 2, we listed a number of warning signs of substance abuse to look for when you suspect someone is using. Then, be willing to ask. Notice, the word is *ask*, not *accuse*. The idea is to express your concern—and then be willing to *listen.*

It's best not to try to carry this kind of burden alone. Talk to a trusted adult, teacher, religious leader, law enforcement officer, doctor, or someone else that can give you support and counsel about what to do.

Then track down local help-lines or recovery programs. If your friend is willing to admit he has a problem, offer to go with him to a group meeting, like AL-ANON.

If at any time your friend appears to have overdosed or is having an adverse reaction to a drug, get medical help immediately. It's an emergency! Your willingness to risk getting help may save your friend's life.

Last, remember that you can't make your friend want to change. Your friend has to come to the decision that he needs help, and then be willing to get it. You can only be there to encourage and support him.

So How About You?

What steps can you take to stay drug free? Try these:

1. Have a plan. Know what you plan to say *ahead of time* if someone hands you a joint or offers you a beer.
2. Think through your reasons for saying "no," and then be honest in talking about them.
3. Be prepared to walk away if you need to. True

friends won't push you into any activity that can harm you.

4. Make plans for the future. Do you want to go to college? Do you want to train for a career? Knowing where you're headed makes it easier to say no to things that could derail your plans.
5. Hang out with substance-free teens.
6. Find a trusted adult who can help you stand your ground.
7. Get fit! Join a health club, Y, or sports team. Exercise regularly.
8. Get involved with drug resistance groups in your area (for example, D.A.R.E.).
9. Volunteer at a local drug clinic, soup kitchen, homeless shelter, or hospital that ministers to substance abusers. Seeing the real-life devastation drug use causes in other people can be a powerful antidrug.
10. Get psychiatric help if you're depressed. Sometimes depression (or other psychiatric disorders) can lead to inappropriate drug use.

The path to substance abuse and addiction *always* begins with a single defining choice. The power to resist or overcome that path is entirely in your hands. It's up to you.

Barbour, Scott, ed. *Alcohol: Opposing Viewpoints*. San Diego, Calif.: Greenhaven, 1998.

Bellenir, Karen. *Drug Information for Teens: Health Tips about the Physical and Mental Effects of Substance Abuse*. Detroit, Mich.: Omnigraphics, 2002.

Columbia University's Health Education Program. *The Go Ask Alice® Book of Answers: A Guide to Good Physical, Sexual, and Emotional Health*. New York: Henry Holt and Company, 1998.

Eller, T. Suzanne. *Real Teens, Real Stories, Real Life*. Tulsa, Okla.: River Oak, 2002.

Graves, Bonnie. *Drug Use and Abuse*. Mankato, Minn.: Capstone Press, 2000.

Hyde, Margaret O., and John F. Setaro, M.D. *Alcohol 101: An Overview for Teens*. Breckenridge, Colo.: 21st Century Books, 1999.

Ketcham, Katherine. *Teens Under the Influence: The Truth About Kids, Alcohol, and Other Drugs—How to Recognize the Problem and What to Do About It*. New York: Ballantine, 2003.

Littell, Mary Ann. *LSD*. Springfield, N. J.: Enslow, 1996.

Masline, Shelagh Ryan. *Drug Abuse and Teens: A Hot Issue*. Berkeley Heights, N. J.: Enslow, 2000.

McGraw, Jay. *Life Strategies for Teens*. New York: Fireside, 2000.

McLaughlin, Miriam Smith and Sandra Peyser Hazouri. *Addiction: The High that Brings You Down.* Berkeley Heights, N. J.: Enslow, 1997.

Pringle, Laurence. *Drinking: A Risky Business.* New York: William Morrow, 1997.

Schleichert, Elizabeth. *Marijuana.* Springfield, N. J.: Enslow, 1996.

Winters, Paul A., ed. *Teen Addiction.* San Diego, Calif.: Greenhaven, 1997.

Al-Anon/Alateen Family Groups
1600 Corporate Landing Parkway
Virginia Beach, VA 23454
(310) 534-1815 (Message Only)
Toll free: (888) 4AL-ANON
www.al-anon.alateen.org

Alcohol and Other Drug Information for Teens
National Children's Coalition
www.child.net/drugalc.htm

Canadian Centre on Substance Abuse
75 Albert Street, Suite 300
Ottawa, ON Canada K1P 5E7
(613) 235-4048
www.ccsa.ca

Centers for Disease Control (CDC) Adolescent and
School Health
HealthyYouth@cdc.gov
www.cdc.gov/nccdphp/dash

D.A.R.E.
Drug Abuse Resistance Education
www.dare.com

D.E.A.L. (Drug Education and Awareness for Life)
Royal Canadian Mounted Police (RCMP)
RCMP deal.org Program
A403-1200 Vanier Parkway
Ottawa, ON, Canada K1A 0R2
(613) 993-4023
info@deal.org
www.deal.org

FOCUS Adolescent Services
(410) 341-4342 or (877) 362-8727
www.focusas.com

For Real (freevibe.com)
www.freevibe.com

Go Ask Alice!
Columbia University's Health Question and Answer
Internet Service
www.goaskalice.columbia.edu

Habit Smart
www.habitsmart.com

National Center for Tobacco-Free Kids
1400 Eye Street, Suite 1200
Washington, DC 20005
(202) 296-5469
tobaccofreekids.org

National Clearinghouse for Alcohol and Drug Information (NCADI)
(800) 729-6686
webmaster@health.org
www.health.org

National Institute on Alcohol Abuse and Alcoholism
(NIAAA)
Willco Building
6000 Executive Boulevard
Bethesda, MD 20892-7003
www.niaaa.nih.gov

National Institute on Drug Abuse (NIDA)
National Institutes of Health
6001 Executive Boulevard, Room 5213
Bethesda, MD 20892-9561
(301) 443-1124
www.drugabuse.gov

NIDA for Teens
teens.drugabuse.gov

NIDA on Steroid Abuse
www.steroidabuse.org

Office of National Drug Control Policy (ONDCP)
Drug Policy Information Clearinghouse
P.O. Box 6000
Rockville, MD 20849–6000
(800) 666-3332
ondcp@ncjrs.org
www.whitehousedrugpolicy.gov

StreetDrugs.Org
Publishers Group, LLC
2805 Alvarado Lane North
Plymouth, MN 55447
(763) 473-0646
info@streetdrugs.org
www.streetdrugs.org

Students Against Destructive Decisions (SADD)
SADD National
Box 800
Marlborough, MA 01752
(877) SADD-INC
www.saddonline.com

TEEN ANON
PO Box 191396
Rincon Station
San Francisco, CA 94119
(510) 464-4677
www.teen-anon.com

Teen Health Centre
1585 Ouellette Ave.
Windsor, ON, Canada N8X 1K5
(519) 253-8481
www.teenhealthcentre.com

Teenage Addicts Can Recover
www.day-by-day.org

Publisher's note:
The Web sites listed on these pages were active at the time of publication. The publisher is not responsible for Web sites that have changed their addresses or discontinued operation since the date of publication. The publisher will review and update the Web sites upon each reprint.

angst A feeling of anxiety or apprehension.

behavioral therapies Method treatments that focus on changing observable behaviors.

bipolar disorder Formerly called manic-depression, a psychological disorder characterized by feelings of extreme highs and tremendous lows.

chronic Lasting a long time or recurring frequently.

dehydration The loss of body fluids; extreme dehydration can lead to death.

entitlement A feeling of being "owed."

euphoria (you-FOR-ee-uh) A feeling of extreme joy.

genes The sequence of nucleotides responsible for the transmission of inheritable characteristics.

illusive Difficult to achieve.

initiatives Procedure allowing a specified number of voters to propose legislation.

instant gratification Immediate satisfaction.

metabolism Chemical changes in a living body that provides the energy needed for vital processes.

methadone A synthetic narcotic often given in the treatment of heroin addiction.

neurological Dealing with the body's nervous system.

obsessive-compulsive disorder A personality disorder characterized by preoccupation with perfection, control, and orderliness.

oppositional defiant disorder A pattern of negative and hostile behavior, characterized by being easily annoyed, being annoying, arguing, and losing one's temper, that lasts for more than six months in a child.

panic attacks Sudden feelings of extreme anxiousness, characterized by rapid heartbeat and shortness of breath.

paranoia (pare-uh-NOY-uh) A feeling of distrust of others, often assigning negative connotations to others' motives.

posttraumatic stress disorder An anxiety disorder caused by extreme physical or mental experiences.

puberty The stage at which one becomes capable of sexual reproduction.

rave An all-night dance party that frequently moves from place to place.

relative Compared with something else.

schizophrenia (skits-oh-FREN-ee-uh) A psychotic disorder characterized by disturbances in one or more major areas of functioning, such as school and interpersonal relations, with symptoms including delusions, hallucinations, and inappropriate affect.

stimulants Chemicals that provoke an increase in action or output.

techno (TEK-no) Electronic dance music, often played at raves.

INDEX

PICTURE CREDITS

Artville pp. 12, 15, 28, 30, 42, 72, 82, 88, 102
BrandX pp. 53, 68, 109
Corel p. 80
Coresample p. 96 (lower image)
DJ Walkingstick p. 96 (upper image)
EyeWire pp. 10, 50
iDream pp. 100, 112
Autumn Libal pp. 37, 38
Masterseries pp. 74, 114
PhotoAlto pp. 16, 21
Photodisc pp. 22, 35, 77
Benjamin Stewart pp. 32, 61, 65, 93
Stockbyte pp. 62, 105

The individuals in these photographs are models,
and the images are for illustrative purposes only.

Joan Esherick is a full-time author, freelance writer, and professional speaker who lives outside of Philadelphia, Pennsylvania, with her husband and three teenagers. She is the author of ten books, including *Our Mighty Fortress: Finding Refuge in God* (Moody Press, 2002), *The Big Picture: The Bible's Story in Thirty Short Scenes*, and multiple books with Mason Crest Publishers. Joan has contributed dozens of articles to national print periodicals and speaks nationwide. For more information about her, you can visit her Web site at www.joanesherick.com.

Mary Ann McDonnell, APRN, BC, is an advanced practice nurse, the director of the clinical trials program in pediatric psychopharmacology research at Massachusetts General Hospital, has a private practice in pediatric psychopharmacology, and is a clinical instructor for Northeastern University and Boston College advanced practice nursing students. Her areas of expertise are bipolar disorder in children and adolescents, ADHD, and depression. Mary Ann is one of a small group of advanced practice nurses working in pediatric psychopharmacology research and practice, who has a national reputation as an expert advanced practice nurse in the field of pediatric bipolar disorder, ADHD, and depression. She sits on the institutional review board and the research education committee at Massachusetts General Hospital and is a lecturer for local and national educational conferences on bipolar disorder, depression, and ADHD.

Dr. Sara Forman graduated from Barnard College and Harvard Medical School. She completed her residency in Pediatrics at Children's Hospital of Philadelphia and a fellowship in Adolescent Medicine at Children's Hospital Boston (CHB). She currently is an attending in Adolescent Medicine at CHB, where she has served as Director of the Adolescent Outpatient Eating Disorders Program for the past nine years. She has also consulted for the National Eating Disorder Screening Project on its high school initiative and has presented at many conferences about teens and eating disorders. In addition to her clinical and administrative roles in the Eating Disorders Program, Dr. Forman teaches medical students and residents and coordinates the Adolescent Medicine rotation at CHB. Dr. Forman sees primary care adolescent patients in the Adolescent Clinic at CHB, at Bentley College, and at the Germaine Lawrence School, a residential school for emotionally disturbed teenage girls.